Tadia A foster

Meticulous Moments *and* Placid Places

Meticulous Moments *and* Placid Places

Tadia A Foster

Kravitz & Sons
INNOVATORS IN PUBLISHING, MARKETING AND ADVERTISING

Kravitz and Sons LLC
204 E Arlington Blvd. Suite B
Greenville, NC 27858

Published by Kravitz and Sons LLC.
ISBN: 979-8-89639-465-5 (sc)
ISBN: 979-8-89639-464-8 (e)

Library of Congress Control Number: 2026901525

In Dedication

My Mother- I love you now and always. All that I am and ever will be, if there be any good in me, is because of my mother.

My Great Aunt Mrs. Yvonne Barracks- Thank you for your sacrifice, taking me in as your own. I love you now and always

Contents

METICULOUS MOMENTS

PLACID PLACES

ACKNOWLEDGEMENTS

I would like to express my gratitude to the staff at WestBow Press. Thank you for your assistance in bringing my project to life.

In recognition of my family who resides in the USA, Canada, Jamaica-West Indies, and United Kingdom-because of you, there is me-Thank you for support. To my mother, for not giving up on me, thank you. To my father, for your strong work ethic and setting a great example for how a man should provide for his family, thank you.

To my friends for their support- thank you. I would like to acknowledge my personal mentor, Mr. and Mrs. Arrasmith, for your support and encouragement. It's my hope that this book warms your soul.

To the English Department and Social Work Department at Southern Adventist University, Thank you for aiding in my development as a fellow professional. I have been able to apply the information that I learned.

To my Professional Mentors and Colleagues, thank you for your support.

To the Most High God and His Son- Yeshua- Jesus Christ, to His People, and those called His name, may this book encourage deeper self-introspection and greater appreciation for what God has created for us to enjoy. My Utmost for His Highest.

INTRODUCTION

Meticuolous moments and Placid places are a collection of free verse poems meant to inspire the imagination. While writing these poems, I thought over my life and the memories that came to mind.

I have meant for the poems to bring back thought provoking notions into the readers mind. It is my hope that these words will inspire, enable, and encourage the reader.

Life if meant to be enjoyed and in this collection of poems, I hope my pleasure in living is brought to the forefront.

Happy reading!

Note to the Reader-

First thank you for purchasing this book.

It is my aim that this collection of free verse poems will inspire a greater contemplation on the importance of life, treasure every breath that we are allowed to enjoy, implore vulnerability of the soul, and exude peace through quiet inner strength.

I invite you to explore your world- the good, the bad, and the beautiful. Peace unto you and yours.

Tadia A Foster

METICULOUS MOMENTS

Kiss in the air

As I leave the evening meeting,
We shake hands goodbye.
Watching your mouth move as you speak,
You bid me a wonderful evening,
The puckering up of your lips,
A kiss through the air you offer.

I ponder to myself,
If you desire to give such affection to me,
Why give it through the air,
What is untouched affection?
How does the one receiving it benefit?

Contemplative Inquiries

Where do you go when you are at the bottom of the mountain?
How do you leap from the base to the pinnacle?
What do you give when near exhaustion?
When is the end truly enough?

Where do you go when at the fork in the road?
How do you determine which path is the correct one to travel on?
What do you gain if all your possessions
can be destroyed in minutes?
When can unanswerable questions cease?

LET GO

I had to let go of what was not
In order to set my soul free.
Holding onto a wishful thought,
My energy becomes deplete.

Our love will never be a reality;
It is only a fateful twist.
Moving on is a decision,
Letting go, the first step.
New journeys to voyage,
My sails are now set.

Leaving you in the past,
A memory on a page.
This is my best way to move forward,
And embrace my new life.

FREE TO LOVE

I am free to love,
No longer am I afraid.
No longer am I in chains.
Transformed energy comes alive within my soul.

What I once considered beneath me,
Now I rise to greet.
Whom I thought was unlovable,
I now embrace.

Renewed vision freed me,
The gatekeeper of division became obsolete.
Free from traditions and code regulations,
Broken down the barriers of isolation,
I am free to love.

Three Women

Strong willed and independent,
Confident intellectualist,
Brave and cautiously optimistic,
Prudent traveler.

Spiritually intrigued and altruistic,
Intuitive visionary,
Secure and joyful smile,
Vigilant traveler.

Composed and open hearted
Rationality tolerant,
Gentle- spirit and passionate,
Adventurous traveler.

My love, My love

I release myself to you,
withholding nothing personal,
My love, My love.

I promise you endless perpetuity,
priceless precious sacrifice,
My love, My love.

I give you an endowment,
my boundless peace,
My love, my love.

DREAMS UNFULFILLED

What happens to a dream that does not come true?
Does it float out into the ocean blue?
Or change colors like fall leaves on trees?
Do dreams wither away and die, or become
part of the Thanksgiving pie?
Is it possible for a dream to rise early and return in the evening?
Will it come down in the form of rain, refreshing the soul?
Are dreams unreached hiding in the starlit sky?
Reminding us to continue trying and not to give up?

Spoken To Me

If I think about the words you said to me,

"You will not make it"
"You are an evil person"
"I will be taking care of you"
"I will disown you"
"I may tell you to separate from us"
"Don't be the embarrassment of the family"

I gained confidence from your adversarial comments,
Deeper respect for myself,
We will never be close,
And you lost the love of a child.

A Mother's Love

Praise God for a mother's love,
An earthly blessing sent from heaven.
Lacking this is like a suckling babe with no milk.
As the sun rises and sets,
day by day,
From the beginning- to the end of the age-
Her love is constant and never loses influence.

Mystifying Box

This item has sides,
It contained personal possessions to its owner,
Should I open it?
After all no is around.
Well maybe a mystery is meant to remain unexplained,
But this desire does not want leave me.

A Short Memoir

From where I was to present day,
Long road have I traveled.

An angry caregiver,
Codependency surrounding me.

Alone within a nuclear group,
As if I was a traveler with suitcase in hand,
journeying to the next destination.

New environment lacking walls of confinement,
at peace with the promise of a greater life,
Ready for the set of challenges ahead.

TO THE FAMILY I NEVER KNEW

It amazes me how I stand amongst my own,
As though I entered the wrong aisle in a grocery store.
Standing here-
wondering how long this time it will last,
Glancing at the walls, staring at the open kitchen,
Wishing for deliverance.

I wonder
Has anyone else ever felt lost around family known?
Lived in the same home, yet we are perfect strangers.
Outside of the home,
our memories are few,
Casual conversations,
nothing beyond surface,
Waiting for a new day.

DREAM GUY

I loved his wooly soft hair,
His muscular arms,
His caramel Honey- kissed skin.

The way his hand felt when he held mine,
The perfect touch.

I loved his smile,
His messy English,
Tree -barked pierced eyes.

WHAT I NEED

When we first met,
I tried to put a damper on our connection.
You agreed we could be friends,
But I knew you wanted more.

Your presence challenges me,
I must put on my adult face.
I am encouraged to grow,
to develop myself into womanhood.

With you there is not much room for child play.
Maybe you are just what I needed?
Gentle strength to challenge my fears,
tender affection to calm my nerves.

REMINISCE

Where did the time go?
Rivers come from my eyes,
I made it to the end-
So I thought…

I never assumed it would end,
This unstable life of over sheltered rules,
social life with few friends,
Only judgmental faces to greet me.

HONEY

Sweet,
Smooth,
Silky,
Butterscotch.

Health-benefiting
Cold soothing,
Bee endorsing,
Tee welcoming.

YOU AND I

You have created a box for me to stay in,
You think no one will harm me in here.

You keep me safe in a clean world,
You mean well by your good intentions.

I am concerned with your expression of love towards me.

WE ARE COOL

We are cool, so you say,
Does that mean we get along just fine?
For those of us who do not use such language,
What am I to get by this phrase?
We both know what happened in the past between us,
Our "friendship" protected by the secrets we share,
That we do not want anyone else to know.
Tell me, how are we cool?

CONTROL THE CLOCK

Have you ever wanted to stop the clock?
To be able to reverse the time or tell it to stop?
Standing here eating breakfast in a hurry,
Trying my best to scurry,
I wish I could control time,
That would ease my mind.
If only minutes could be put on hold,
Or tell hours stop cold,
That way I would never be out of luck.

Tick, Tock, Tick, Tock,
If only I could control the clock.

ALONE

Stare into oblivion,
Wait for the meal,
Embrace the nutritional aroma.

Fingers tap the key chain,
Filled chairs with tables,
People discussing their days.

How unique to feel-
Alone in a room full of people,
Empty line of seats now warmed.

Our Secret World

Our secret world.

We enter it every time we meet
No need for lock and key.
We do not even have to speak.
The gaze we share are our most precious points.
Looking at each other's faces,
Our thoughts pass with great flight.

No need for porter or security,
safely lodge, together our home.
The intimacy we have,
only our hearts will truly recognize.
What we gain grows deeper day by day.

Our secret world.

STANDING THERE

I see you standing there,
I ponder what is on your mind,
Your face seems to choke your smile,
Your eyes gaze aimlessly around the room.

I wonder if you know your own beauty,
Or if anyone said anything kind to you today,
What is it that your life lacks?
Could I be the answer to your need of adventure?

PLACID PLACES

ONE WRONG MOVE

One wrong move,
Cost me more than I ever dreamed.

If I simply had sat with my friends that day,
I would not have this regret.

What started out as a decent friendship,
Soon became the main source of my pain

Trying to leave was difficult.
So now I am left to ponder why I chose to interact.

Looking back, I see how one wrong move
Gave me more than what I bargained more.

EMPTY HOUSE

Extravagant driveway with red bricks.
Blinds open for one to peak through.
I walk up the extensive steps
and enter the main room.

Chair pillows motionless as though untouched for years.
House stands still as if no people were here,
Window panes filled with copious amounts of dust.
Outside empty but the inside is dead.

Monotony

Stare at the wall,
Hope it would jump.
Listen for clatter.

Minutes pass like days,
Seconds from sixty to eighty-six thousand.
Quite a leap through time.

So, this is how it must be,
Who would have guessed?
Schedule-less days so tedious.

PASSAGE PROCESS

I float on air,
transient though discreet darkness.
Suddenly, a figure appears,
walking an andante speed.
Hush! What is this I hear?
Startled, I close my eyes into a
soporific sweet night.

WET

Nothing beats being wet.

The opposite of secure and warm.
Soaked, dripping, or drenched.

Water sticking on your skin,
Like fresh dew on morning grass.

Moisture dangling from strands of damp hair.
Bodies move effortlessly through much free weight.

Nothing beats being wet.

Hole in the Stone

Passing by on the highway,
I noticed a hole in the stone.
It was circular and carved out neatly.
I pondered if someone lived there,
A person who made this their home.

Free air conditioning,
shelter from snow and rain.
I accept that the hole in the stone
serves it purpose of accommodation,
to assist those who cannot afford otherwise.

Island Dreams

Tropical breezes,
Sea blue sky,
Rain water buckets,
Mangoes, breadfruit, saltfish, jerk chicken.

Grill windows,
Lime green grass,
Dirt road games,
Beaches, churches, ocean view homes, fresh markets.

View of the Mediterranean

Blue-green water,
Narrow city street.

Windows open with small gardens in the sills.
Children running after fresh fowl.

People bustling to and fro,
All carrying important belongings.

Amongst the busy sound,
A bird chirps from a nearby tree

River Comments

River water gushing,
Motionless rocks,
Leaves silently applauding its speed.
Insects roaming through,
Trying to find their place, amongst trickles of dirt.
Amidst this soundless parade,
Peace enters my heart.
Gazing at the green canopy above—
I am reminded of God's eternal love.

Rain Thoughts

Pitter, Patter, Pitter, Patter
How small drops can make such music!

I hear them fall and think of happy times.
Warm blankets, stories, and hot cocoa come to mind.

As I gaze through a window,
Watch the drops fall,
I think who would ever want to miss this sight—
Raindrops falling through the day and night.

Invasive Procedure

Blank walls,
sterile instruments,
soundless noise,
few people,
eyes closed,
dream world,
one hour.

BANQUET OF THE YEAR

Pumpkin colored tablecloth,
clear kissed glasses,
purple juice, smooth on the stomach.
People gather around me,
near and far they come to this occasion.
Mouth moist, nostrils open,
time for the meal of the year,
fork of gratitude and knife of prayers.

I begin to indulge.

AIDE DAYS

Several demand my attention,
my two hands lack a break.
06:59, one minute till freedom.
I sprint down the foyer,
grateful to see the sunlight's
gaze through the entrance window.
I lift my head in contentment,
I assisted the vulnerable today.

Moon Talk

Although we are in different corners of the world,
Staring into the sky,
I gaze upon the moon-
Our uniting point.

Indigo embellishes this moment,
I stand alone feeling your greeting,
Embracing your presence,
The gaze from the moon gives me comfort.

I will see you again... tonight.

OCEAN VIEW

Birds dipping their mouths' in to get a charming taste,
Air spreading out its hands to meet its Maker,
Sand extending itself to an unknown number,
Palm tree swaying to its own song,
Whales jumping to their own harmony,
Waves joining forces and increase in sound,
And I am enjoying the tranquility of perfect melody.

AWAKEN

I thought my mind left me,
Like as if the dream was real,
A nightmare with wheels.

Trembling in sheets,
I turn on my light,
Confirming that the ordeal is over.

I.

Trees red,
Leaves fall from someone's head.
Standing amazed everything around,
Like as if someone famous has come to town.

What time is it now,
Is the feeling expressed by your brow?
Tis fall, the season of chill,
Winter on its way, to do as it will.

II.

Blanket of white covering the earth
Invisible clouds
Piercing cold -if left alone one would suffer

Trees stand motionless.
Empty wind
Sucks life out of transient beauty.

Lake of ice -a trap for silver blades.
Iced lanes
Neighborhoods still though a burglar was visiting.

III.

Alive again,
Renewed vision lives.
Blood pumping through my veins,
Winter has passed, a fresh day awaits!

Flowers blossom, insects hustle quietly,
Birds serenade, leaves applaud,
Wind adds his encore.
It's time.

IV.

Days go nowhere,
As if to run an endless race.
Time passes quietly,
Slow is the new fast.
Cumulus clouds hide the sun,
Plenty of blue to gaze into.
Insects fight over fresh skin,
Grass provide blanket of empathy.

About the Author

Tadia A Foster is a native or Aurora, Illinois. She was born to Caribbean parents and is a first-generation immigrants' offspring in the USA. She recently graduated from Southern Adventist University with a MSW in 2019. In her spare time, she enjoys reading, nature walks, and making Caribbean food. Please follow her on Twitter and alexandriatadia. wordpress.com.

www.ingramcontent.com/pod-product-compliance
Lightning Source LLC
Chambersburg PA
CBHW051556120626
46551CB00013B/1536